# Mysterious Encounters

# Time Travel

## by Stuart A. Kallen

**KIDHAVEN PRESS**
*A part of Gale, Cengage Learning*

GALE
CENGAGE Learning™

Detroit • New York • San Francisco • New Haven, Conn • Waterville, Maine • London

GALE
CENGAGE Learning™

LIBRARY OF CONGRESS CATALOGING-IN-PUBLICATION DATA

Kallen, Stuart A., 1955-
    Time travel / by Stuart A. Kallen.
       p. cm. -- (Mysterious encounters)
    Includes bibliographical references and index.
    ISBN 978-0-7377-4573-3 (hardcover)
    1. Time travel--Juvenile literature. 2. Fourth dimension (Parapsychology)--Juvenile literature. I. Title.
    BF1045.T55K35 2009
    001.9--dc22
                                                                          2009014517

KidHaven Press
27500 Drake Rd.
Farmington Hills, MI 48331

ISBN-13: 978-0-7377-4573-3
ISBN-10: 0-7377-4573-8

Printed in the United States of America
1 2 3 4 5 6 7 13 12 11 10 09

Printed by Bang Printing, Brainerd, MN, 1st Ptg., 10/2009

# Contents

# Chapter 1

# The Riddle of Time

The year was 1932 and two newspaper reporters were covering a story in the shipyards of Hamburg, Germany. Journalist J. Bernard Hutton and photographer Joachim Brandt had taken a tour of the facility where ships were built and were preparing to leave. Suddenly the men heard the drone of airplanes approaching. Looking to the sky and seeing many fighter planes, the men thought they were seeing a practice drill. But the planes were decorated with the British flag. Then the whistle of falling bombs and the crackle of antiaircraft gunfire rose above the whining engine noise.

Thinking they were about to die, Hutton and Brandt rushed to their car. Within seconds, however, the airplanes were gone and silence fell on the landscape. The shipyards had returned to their normal appearance. There were no airplanes, bombs, or bullets.

Later Brandt developed the pictures he had taken during the air raid. They showed only peaceful shipyards with no sign of the airplanes. The men were mystified. Then in 1943 during World War II, both Hutton and Brandt were stationed at the shipyard. While they were there, Great Britain's Royal Air Force bombed the facility and destroyed the Hamburg shipyards in a fiery inferno. Hutton and Brandt came to believe that in 1932 they had traveled through time into the future. What they saw was the event that would take place in 1943.

## Excellent Adventures

The story of the Hamburg air raid is among dozens told by people who believe they have traveled through time. Although no one has ever proved that they actually visited the past or the future, stories about time travel have fascinated people for years.

One of the most famous stories about a person who visits the future was written by British author H.G. Wells in 1895. Wells' book, *The Time Machine*, is about a man known only as the Time Traveler. He builds a machine that takes him into the future.

The Time Traveler's time machine takes him to the year 802,701. Here he finds a race of people,

An illustration from *The Time Machine* by H.G. Wells shows the Time Traveler meeting the Eloi people.

called the Eloi. These beautiful, peaceful people are tormented by Morlocks, monsters that live underground. The Morlocks soon steal the time machine. The Time Traveler must enter the Morlocks' underground lair and fight the fiends to get his machine back.

*The Time Machine* was made into several movies, one in 1960 and the other in 2002. Countless other films, such as *Planet of the Apes,, Bill and Ted's Excellent Adventure, Back to the Future*, and *12 Monkeys* are also about time travelers.

These films are considered **science fiction**; that is, made-up stories loosely based on scientific concepts. But there are **physicists** who believe time travel might be possible someday. As physicist Jenny Randles says, "The charming fiction of H.G. Wells . . . has morphed into fevered debates between world-renowned researchers arguing over how [a time machine] can be made to work."[1]

## What Time Is It?

The time of day is a man-made invention that has nothing to do with the past or the future. Clocks simply tick off seconds, minutes, and hours. But they do not define what time is or what it is made of.

# The Fourth Dimension

In *The Time Machine* H.G. Wells describes time as the fourth **dimension**. As an author with scientific training, Wells describes what many physicists of his day had recently discovered. The concept of three dimensions is easily understood by looking at a box which has height, width, and depth. With three dimensions (height, width, and depth), the box exists in space. But it also exists in time.

The box was created at some point in time. It might have been created minutes, hours, days, weeks, months, or years ago. And the box will someday crumble into dust and cease to exist. Scientists call time the fourth dimension. Therefore, the box—and everything else in the universe—exists in time and space.

Space is easy to understand. A person walks in a hallway, a car is driven on a road, and birds fly through the sky. They are all moving through space and can move one direction and back again. However, time is harder to define. Clocks and calendars can measure periods of time, but they do not describe what it is. They only provide numbered markers on an endless one-way path for the past, present, and future.

While time cannot be seen, touched, or defined, its effects are clear. A small maple seed grows into a tall oak tree over time. The fresh paint on a building weathers and peels as time passes, and a bolt of lightning flashes for a second and disappears for-

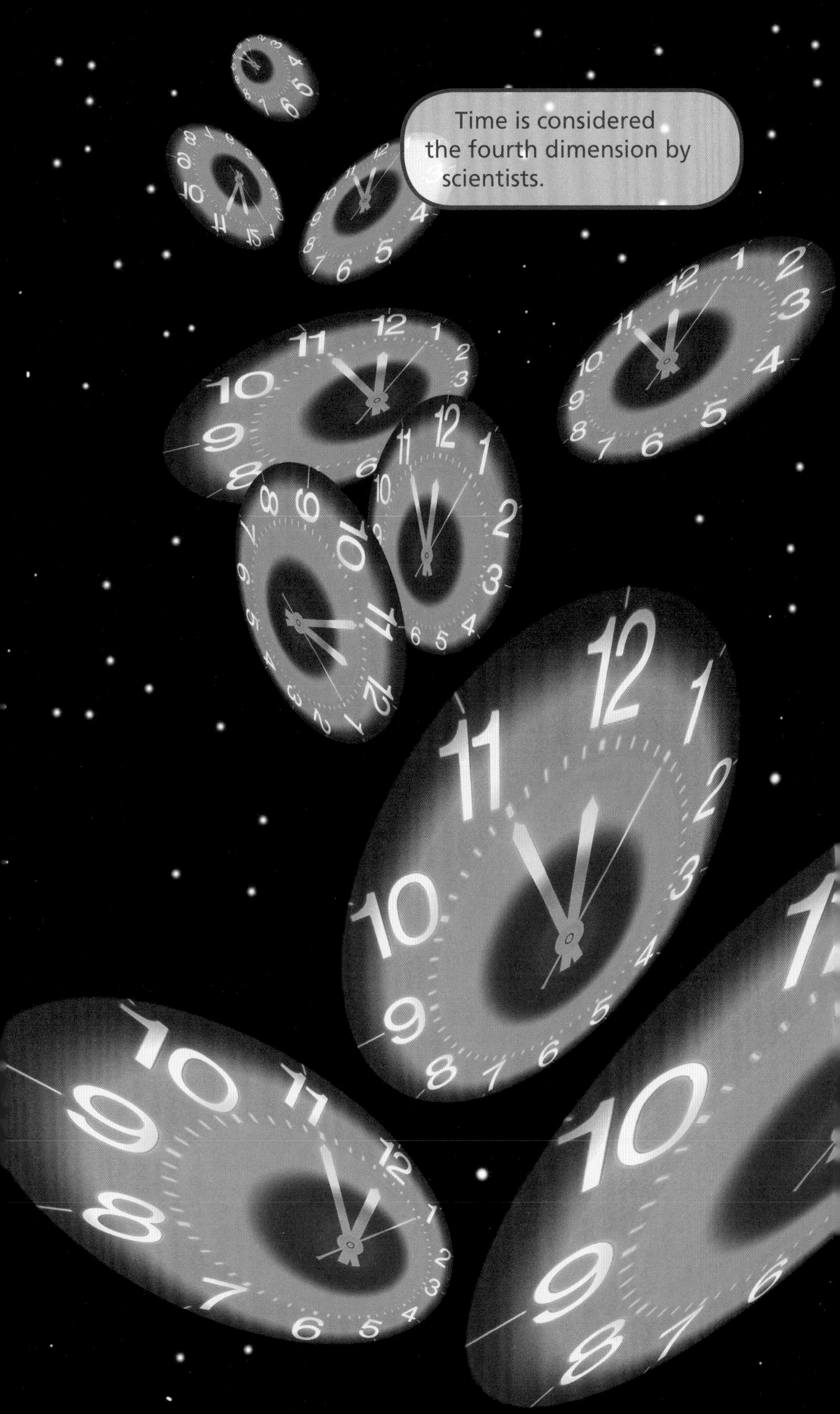

Time is considered the fourth dimension by scientists.

ever. The passage of time is easy to see in humans. Tiny babies grow into tall teenagers, who grow into adults. Bodies age, skin eventually wrinkles, and hair turns gray as adults grow old.

# The Grandfather Paradox

The theory of time travel is based on complicated ideas, and there are many unknown factors. One of the biggest questions is whether a person who goes back in time could change history.

For example, a person who believes Abraham Lincoln was the greatest president in history might want to return to the 1860s. The person could then warn Lincoln that he was going to be assassinated by John Wilkes Booth on April 15, 1865.

If a time traveler stopped Lincoln's murder from happening in 1865, would he change history for all the years that followed? This would make today different than it is, so changing history would probably be impossible. Because, if Abraham Lincoln never died, then someone from the future would not have to return to the past to warn him about being killed. This idea is known as the grandfather **paradox**. A paradox is an idea or situation that seems to be at odds with itself and seems impossible.

The grandfather paradox supposes that a time traveler goes back to the past and kills his own grandfather. This may be by accident or on purpose. Either way, the question remains. If the time traveler kills his grandfather, how could the time traveler ever have been born? Therefore the grand-

Abraham Lincoln can be used as an example to illustrate the grandfather paradox, which is an idea or situation that is at odds with itself and seems impossible.

father cannot be killed by his own grandson.

## The Parallel Universe

Those who study time travel have developed a theory that solves the grandfather paradox. Some

## Crowds of Time Tourists

**"Perhaps one or two time travelers could blend in with local crowds at historical events, but if many time travelers had been present, surely the historical record would document this."**

Clifford A. Pickover, *Time: A Traveler's Guide*. New York: Oxford University Press, 1998, p. 81.

physicists believe that time travelers enter a parallel universe. It is exactly the same as this world, but its history changes the minute the time traveler arrives.

When history is changed in a parallel universe, it creates what scientists call a split-time track. On one track the universe continues as it always has. On the other track the time traveler can alter history by, perhaps, killing his grandfather.

With the split-time track, the grandfather only dies in one universe. The time traveler could then exist only in the parallel universe of the past, unable to return to the universe he started in.

A parallel universe may be difficult to understand. But physicists will have to figure out such concepts in order to figure out if time travel is possible.

# Chapter 2

# Time Slips

ost time travel tales involve unusual machines that take people backward or forward in time. But some people believe that time travel is made possible by something called a time slip. It is an event that cannot be explained by natural laws. A time slip is described as **supernatural**, like ghosts or magical spells.

Time slips have been used in many stories. In the 1969 novel *Slaughterhouse-Five*, by Kurt Vonnegut Jr., the main character, Billy Pilgrim, becomes unstuck in time. Time slips allow Pilgrim to jump back and forth in his life, sometimes living as a young man, other times living as an old man.

In the world of television, a 1970 show called

*Timeslip* was based on two children who could skip through time. They were able to visit themselves as adults or see their parents as children.

## A Time Slip in France

In 1901 two British women, Charlotte Anne Moberly and Eleanor Jourdain, claimed to have really experienced a time slip.

They were on vacation near Paris, France. On August 10, they visited the gardens of a small castle called Petit Trianon at the Palace of Versailles. Petit Trianon had been the private home of French queen Marie Antoinette in the 18th century. The queen

This painting depicts a garden party at the Petit Trianon, the site of a time slip by two British tourists.

often spent time there, overseeing the planting of lush gardens and dining and dancing with French nobles. Life was good until 1793 when Marie Antoinette was murdered by French revolutionaries.

More than a century after the queen's death, Moberly and Jourdain became lost on a visit to the Palace of Versailles. Missing their destination, they turned down an unmarked lane where things seemed odd and out of place.

## Different Recollections

Suddenly the day turned dreary and the two women experienced feelings of depression. Then they saw several men wearing the formal uniforms of palace groundskeepers from the 18th century. Moberly later described them as "very dignified officials, dressed in long greyish green coats with small three-cornered hats."[2]

The women asked for directions and the men pointed in the direction of Petit Trianon. Jourdain later recalled seeing a cottage along the road with a girl and woman in the doorway. The woman was holding a jug out for the girl. Jourdain said the scene looked like a painting; the two French peasants looked like a living picture. Moberly said she did not see the living picture or the cottage but felt a change in the air.

As they continued walking, Moberly and Jourdain came to a garden where they saw a man in a cloak and large hat. Moberly described his face as "most repulsive . . . its expression odious [revolting]. His complexion was dark and rough."[3] Jour-

## Seeing Into the Future

One episode of the 1970 children's TV show *Timeslip* accidentally predicted the future with some accuracy. The two main characters, Simon and Liz, are transported through time to 1990. Because science has been misused, the climate of Earth is at risk. In an eerie prediction about global warming, which was unknown at the time, the show predicted that Earth will face destruction from increasing weather-related heat.

A painting of Marie Antoinette. Moberly recognized the woman she had seen at the Petit Trianon as Marie Antoinette from looking at old paintings.

dain described him as repulsive and evil looking, with a face scarred by smallpox, and wearing a large Spanish-style sombrero hat.

The women walked on, crossing a bridge that took them to the gardens of Petit Trianon. There Moberly saw a lady with long, light-colored hair, wearing an old-fashioned summer dress and a large white hat. She was sitting in the grass and drawing on a pad. But Jourdain did not see the woman. Walking on, Moberly and Jourdain entered the small castle where they found a party in progress. The people there were dressed like French nobility from the 18th century.

The women toured the house and eventually returned home to England. After discussing the odd afternoon, they decided to write separate accounts of what happened. They studied several old paintings and Moberly realized that the woman she had seen in the grass looked like Marie Antoinette. The

## A Costume Party

Critics of the Moberly-Jourdain time slip incident explain that a French poet named Robert de Montesquiou lived near Petit Trianon. He often gave costume parties where people dressed like French royalty to entertain guests. Moberly and Jourdain may have accidentally wandered into such a party. There they saw a local woman dressed like Marie Antoinette, while Montesquiou was posing as her friend, the Comte de Vaudreuil.

repulsive man that both women had seen looked like paintings of the Comte de Vaudreuil, a man who was friends with Antoinette.

Ten years after their visit, Moberly and Jourdain described their experiences in a book called *An Adventure*. To avoid ridicule, they published the book under the names Elizabeth Morison and Frances Grant. Their claim that they had seen Marie Antoinette caused an uproar, and **skeptics** criticized the book. But Moberly and Jourdain believed that they had fallen into a time slip. They declared their story to be true until their deaths many years later. Whether or not the women actually traveled back to a time to see Marie Antoinette and her friends, remains a mystery.

## Slip Along the Highway

A lonely road was the scene of a more recent time slip that two men say they experienced on October 20, 1969. The men, known only as L.C. and Charlie, were driving on a clear, crisp fall afternoon along Highway 167 in southwestern Louisiana about 15 miles (24km) from Lafayette.

There were few cars on the highway, but L.C. and Charlie spotted an antique car cruising slowly ahead of them. The car was turtle shaped, large, and rounded like the cars that were made before World War II. But it was in perfect condition. Charlie, who was driving, prepared to pass the antique car, which was moving very slowly down

A rural highway in Louisiana—much like this one—was the site of a possible instance of time travel.

the road. Pulling up close to the old car, the men noticed that the year on the large, orange license plate said 1940.

As Charlie pulled alongside the antique car, L.C. noticed it was being driven by a young woman in a fur coat, wearing an old-style hat with a feather. Next to her, a small child, also wearing a heavy winter coat and hat, was standing on the seat. The men were puzzled since the temperature was about 60°F (16°C). The people in the old car were overdressed for the weather.

The men became troubled when they saw terror on the woman's face. She looked lost, constantly turning her head back and forth as if searching for something. L.C. lowered his window and asked the woman if she needed help. She moved her head up and down, indicating "yes." He yelled and motioned for her to pull over to the side of the road. With her window rolled up, the woman seemed to have extreme difficulty understanding him.

## Disappeared Without a Trace

Finally the old car pulled over to the side of the road, and Charlie pulled over and stopped in front of it. When the men looked back, the car was gone. The woman and her child had disappeared. There were no other roads where the woman could have turned, and no car was in the ditch by the side of the road.

Charlie and L.C. were mystified. They spent the next hour walking along the road looking for the mysterious old car and its occupants. The men never forgot the incident, and L.C. told a journalist about it in 1988. The men came to believe that the woman had temporarily slipped into the future. One minute she was driving down the Louisiana highway in 1940, the next second she was in 1969. She must have been startled when she saw Charlie's 1969 Chevy. To her, the long, low car covered with chrome would have looked quite strange. When the car disappeared from 1969, it may have slipped back to 1940. Or else the woman and her child may be unstuck in time. They could have disappeared from their own era, and are skipping through time in the old car, driving rural highways and searching for a way back home.

# Chapter 3

# Voices from the Future

In May 2005 a group of physics students at the Massachusetts Institute of Technology (MIT) held a Time Traveler Convention. The purpose of the convention was so "time travelers from all eras could meet at a specific place at a specific time, and they could make as many repeat visits as they wanted."[4] In order to invite people from the future, students were urged to write "details [of the convention] down on a piece of . . . paper, and slip them into obscure books in academic libraries! [Or] carve them into a clay tablet!"[5]

The Time Traveler Convention was a huge success, and tickets quickly sold out. All of the attendees, however, were from the present. No one from

Two students attend the Time Traveler Convention held at the Massachusetts Institute of Technology (MIT) in 2005.

the past or the future showed up. The event was covered in the *New York Times* and *Boston Globe* newspapers and even mentioned on the comedy TV show *Saturday Night Live*.

While the Time Traveler Convention was held for fun, the entrance fees were used for a scholarship program. There have been cases, however, of people being serious about being from the future. They said they came to help people in the present.

## A Time-Traveling Soldier

One of the most recent cases of a supposed visitor from the future concerns John Titor. Calling himself Titor or Timetravel_0, he began posting on several Internet bulletin boards in November 2000.

John Titor claimed to have time-traveled to the past in order to retrieve a 1975 model of an IBM computer (similar to the one shown here) needed to fix a computer virus in the year 2036.

His earliest postings showed pictures of what he said was his time machine, along with the operations manual. This prompted people to ask questions. Titor then began providing answers about life in the future.

In his posts, Titor stated that he was an American soldier living on a military base in Tampa, Florida, in the year 2036. As part of his duties, he was assigned to a government time-travel project. He was sent back to 1975 to retrieve an old-style IBM 5100 computer. This was supposedly needed in 2036 to fix ultramodern computers that were infected with a virus. Titor said he was picked for the mission because his grandfather was involved in inventing and programming the 5100. In his bulletin-board posts Titor said he was "stopping over" in 2000 and 2001 for personal reasons. He was trying to collect old family photographs.

## A Bleak Future

As unlikely as Titor's story seemed, he made even more fantastic claims. He said his photographs had been destroyed in a violent war that reached its climax in 2015. At that time, Titor said Russia launched a nuclear strike against cities in the United States, Europe, and China. The nuclear bombs destroyed most of those nations and killed billions of people.

## A One-Way Ride to the Future

"[Once] you've made a time machine you can never use it to go backward in time. . . . There is no way I can use it to travel back to the age of the dinosaurs or even back to the time of my own birth because I didn't make the time machine until recently."

Quoted in PBS, "Time Travel," television episode of the series *NOVA*, airdate October 12, 1999, PBS, www.pbs.org/wgbh/nova/transcripts/2612time.html.

After the war, the capital of the United States was moved to Omaha, Nebraska, one of the few cities left untouched. The environment, however, was contaminated by radiation and disease. The huge farms that supplied food to grocery stores were gone. Survivors grew their own food and raised livestock for meat. Speaking of the postwar world of 2036, Titor says:

> The people that survived grew closer together. Life is centered on the family and then the community. I cannot imagine living even a few hundred miles away from my parents. There is no large industrial complex creating masses of useless food and recreational items. Food and livestock is grown and sold locally. People spend much more time reading and talking together face to face. Religion is taken seriously and everyone can multiply and divide in their heads.[6]

## Titor Disappears

On March 21, 2001, John Titor said he was leaving and returning to 2036. After that, he was never heard from again. Many who read his detailed posts were convinced he was a time traveler from the future. However, it was not long before his story began to unravel. Titor said the great war of 2015 began as a civil war in the United States in 2004. He also said the country would be divided into five

Titor's failure to mention the September 11, 2001 attack on the World Trade Center is one reason people did not believe he traveled through time.

## Fake Photos?

**Photographer Michael Taylor studied Billy Meier's photos of the future and decided they were fake. He writes,**

> One of Meier's photographs, where he allegedly traveled into the future aboard a Pleiadian Beamship to photograph the aftermath of [an] earthquake in San Francisco showing the toppled Trans-America building, turned out to be a realistic looking painting from a geology magazine article about earthquakes.

Michael Taylor, "Billy Meier Exposed!" www.geocities.com/area51/corridor/8148/scam.html.

different regions with five different presidents by 2008. As everyone knows, 2004 and 2008 have come and gone and these things did not happen.

Titor also failed to mention the September 11, 2001, terrorist attacks on the United States. And he never wrote about the wars in Afghanistan and Iraq or the ongoing war with terrorists. These are significant events in history that someone from the future ought to know about. Although he did not mention these events, believers say that Titor's other predictions will come true even if the dates are inaccurate. The debate continues in several Internet forums as people still wonder why John Titor was online and whether or not he really was a time traveler from a very different future.

## Beamships and Seaquakes

Titor is not the only time traveler who describes the future. A Swiss man named Billy Meier also claims to have knowledge of supposed future events.

Meier lives in the present. But he says he was taken into the future by space aliens, called Plejaren. They first visited him in 1942 when he was five years old. Meier's contact with the humanlike **extraterrestrials** (ETs) continued off and on for more than 30 years. In 1975 Meier says the Plejarens took him for a ride into the future in one of their spaceships. He called it a beamship, because it looked like a beam of light.

Meier says he was taken to an unknown time

Billy Meier took this photo of an alien spaceship that he claimed took him into the future.

in the future immediately after a massive earthquake struck the West Coast of the United States. The huge trembler was centered in the ocean and generated a gigantic wave, called a tsunami. Meier referred to the sea-based earthquake, or seaquake, in a 2005 statement he made about the destructive force:

> According to our preview [of the future] there will be a seaquake . . . in the region of the North Pacific not far from the American coast, from Portland to the south of California. . . . As a result there will be a gigantic fault [crack in the earth] . . . when as never before a seaquake-tsunami will spread in a ring . . . and produce immense devastation on the main land and on the islands, which will cost many human lives.[7]

## Photos of the Future?

There is nothing unusual about predicting a huge earthquake on the West Coast. Scientists have long said such an event will happen someday. But Meier claims to have visited San Francisco, California, on a beamship after the earthquake and photographed the destruction.

The time traveler published eleven photos of scenes, such as the landmark TransAmerican Tower lying in ruins and futuristic cars lying in the rubble. Meier also has dozens of pictures of the aliens who

An Indonesian man walks through rubble following a devastating tsunami in 2004. Meier claimed to have seen similar devastation in his travels to the future caused by a seaquake hitting the west coast of the United States.

took him into the future. However, research photographer Michael Taylor says Meier's pictures are fake, and "the photograph of the beautiful . . . [alien woman] turned out to be a photocopy of a model from a Sears Catalog."[8] Nevertheless, Meier has made a good living selling books, videos, and other items dealing with his supposed trips into the future on alien spaceships.

Meier heads a group of dedicated believers in Switzerland who do not doubt his tales of time travel. Taylor, however, believes otherwise writing, "The evidence is overwhelming that the whole Billy Meier story is unquestionably, absolutely, completely and totally 100% BOGUS. Case Closed!"[9]

# Chapter 4

# Building a Time Machine

Most stories about time travel involve special machines that transport people into the past or future. But in the 1950s, an Italian monk named Pellegrino Ernetti said he made a machine that allowed people to see into the past. Father Ernetti called his machine a "chronovisor," an Italian word that means "time viewer."

Ernetti's machine did not allow people to physically travel into the past. According to Ernetti, one could, however, view images of past events on a special screen. Using his chronovisor, Ernetti said he watched a speech being made by French ruler

Scenen aus Napoleons Leben.

Uebergang über den St. Bernhard

am 15ᵗᵉ Mai 1800

Among the historical events Ernetti claimed to have witnessed with his chronovisor was a speech by Napoléon Bonaparte in 1800.

Napoléon Bonaparte in 1800. Ernetti also claimed to have watched a play performed in 169 B.C. at a public square called the Roman Forum. And in 1972 Ernetti produced a screen shot from the chronovisor that supposedly showed Christ during his crucifixion. When the picture was published in an Italian weekly magazine, it created a major sensation.

## Like an Old-Style Television

The story of the chronovisor began with the invention of the atom bomb in the 1940s. Italian-born physicist Enrico Fermi worked on the atom bomb for the United States. In the 1950s, German-born

Enrico Fermi sits at a control panel. Ernetti claimed that Fermi was among the acclaimed scientists who helped him develop the chronovisor.

rocket scientist Wernher von Braun developed long-range missiles with nuclear warheads. Like these two men, Ernetti also had a degree in physics. He stated that Fermi, Braun, and twelve other scientists worked with him to invent the chronovisor.

The machine looked and worked like an old-style television. The screen was a large picture tube, and it was contained in a heavy wooden cabinet with an antenna made from unknown metals. Beneath the screen there were controls that allowed the operator to select the time and location of events to be viewed. The events then played out on the screen like a TV show.

Ernetti said his time machine worked, because people in the past left behind invisible sound and light waves. The chronovisor used microwave energy to pick up and decode these electric and magnetic waves. The chronovisor "read" the waves and reproduced them as audio and video images on the screen. However, the machine could not see into the future because upcoming events were not yet formed. Their energy did not yet exist.

## A Mythical Machine

Pellegrino Ernetti's chronovisor is described in the 2002 book, *The Vatican's New Mystery* by French priest and paranormal author François Brune. Brune says that Ernetti told him about the chronovisor in 1964. However, Ernetti said that the pope had become concerned that the time viewer could be used for ungodly purposes. Therefore, the Vatican, which governs the Catholic Church, ordered Ernetti to break the chronovisor into pieces. The parts were to be scattered in different locations throughout the world so the time machine could never be used again.

Brune was completely convinced that Ernetti's story was true. But in 1994, while on his deathbed, Ernetti confessed to Brune that the chronovisor never existed. Ernetti also said the photo of Christ was a "lie." Indeed, after it was published, experts

## Airplanes and Time Travel

The faster a person moves through space, the slower time passes for them. Therefore, people on airplanes moving 600 miles per hour (966kmph) age slightly less than people on the ground. If someone lived on an airplane for 100 years, he or she would be younger than people on the ground by about one ten-thousandth of a second.

quickly discovered the photo of a bearded Christ gazing upward to heaven was that of a wood carving by sculptor Lorenzo Coullaut Valera. Brune believes that Ernetti was pressured to make a false confession by the Vatican to cover up the existence of the machine. This has led some people to believe that the disappearance of the chronovisor is part of a scheme, or conspiracy. Those who accept the conspiracy theory say the Vatican ordered the destruction of the chronovisor because it might have disproved certain events in the *Bible*.

## Space-Time Continuum

The truth of the chronovisor will never be known. But most physicists believe that it is impossible for a machine to take someone into the past. This is because time machines did not exist in the past. Therefore, a machine cannot go where it does not exist. As the narrator of the *NOVA* television episode "Time Travel" states, physics "forbids one of the most beloved [situations] of science fiction from ever happening because you cannot go back [in time] before . . . the time machine was made."[10] However, physicists do believe that a time machine might be able to transfer people from the present into the future. As physicist Paul Davies says, "traveling forward in time is easy enough."[11]

This belief is based on a theory by Albert Einstein, the physicist whose theories led to the invention of the atom bomb. Einstein said that time is the fourth dimension of the universe. The other three dimensions—height, length, and width—are of space. But time cannot exist without space and

A scene from the 1979 science fiction movie *Time After Time*. Most physicists believe that the type of time travel to the past shown in most science fiction movies will never be possible.

space cannot exist without time. Einstein called the relationship between time and space the space-time **continuum**.

A continuum is a link between two things. They blend together so seamlessly that it is impossible to tell where one begins and the other ends. That is the relationship between space and time.

## The Twin Paradox

Someone who wanted to build a time machine would have to find a way to break through the tight connection between time and space. To do so they would have to build a spaceship that traveled close to the speed of light, which is 186,000 feet per second (56,693mps).

A ship traveling that fast appears to be moving at a crawl to someone who is standing on Earth. Einstein called this slowing of time due to motion time **dilation**. To an astronaut on the spaceship, however, time on Earth speeds up.

Einstein explained time travel into the future with what he called the twin paradox. Suppose there are twins named Sally and Sam who are ten years old. Sally boards a rocket ship and travels into space close to the speed of light. Sam stays at home on Earth. While rocketing through space, Sally checks off one year on her calendar before returning to Earth. However, on Earth, time would appear to be flying by.

When Sally gets back to Earth and steps out of

her spaceship, she finds that her brother has aged ten years during the year she flew at the speed of light. Sam is now twenty years old while Sally is only eleven. Because she was traveling at 186,000 feet per second (56,693mps), Sally leaped nine years into Earth's future.

## Nanoseconds in the Future

The twin paradox has been proved with extremely accurate timepieces, called atomic clocks. These clocks can measure time down to a **nanosecond**, which equals one billionth of one second. An atomic clock was placed on a space shuttle traveling at 17,500 miles per hour (28,164kmh). When the shuttle returned to Earth, its atomic clock was a few nanoseconds slower than a similar clock on the ground.

Time moved faster on Earth than it did for those moving quickly through space. The shuttle astronauts had traveled a few billionths of a second into the future when they landed back on Earth. If they

Atomic clocks, such as this one at the U.S. Naval Observatory, can measure time to the nanosecond.

# Clocks and Rockets

The PBS series *NOVA* explains time dilation using atomic clocks in the program "Einstein's Big Idea":

> Imagine you're standing on Earth holding a clock. Your friend is in a rocket zooming past you at nearly 186,000 miles per second . . . also holding a clock. If you could see your friend's clock, you'd notice that it seems to be moving a lot more slowly than yours. Your friend, on the other hand, thinks . . . your clock on the ground seems to be moving very fast.

"NOVA: Einstein's Big Idea," DVD, directed by Gary Johnstone, PBS, 2005, ww.pbs.org/wgbh/nova/einstein/hotsciencetwin.

had been traveling the speed of light, 186,000 feet per second (56,693mps), the effect would be much more drastic.

No one has invented a way for people to travel at the speed of light, but scientists are working on it. Until then, people will have to experience time travel through fantastic stories in books and movies.

# Notes

## Chapter 1: The Riddle of Time

1. Jenny Randles, *Breaking the Time Barrier*. New York: Paraview Pocket Books, 2005, p. 12.

## Chapter 2: Time Slips

2. Quoted in Terry Castle, *The Female Thermometer: Eighteenth-Century Culture and the Invention of the Uncanny*. Oxford: Oxford University Press, 1995, p. 193.

3. Quoted in "Moberly-Jourdain Incident," AbsoluteAstronomy.com, www.absoluteastronomy.com/topics/Moberly-Jourdain_incident.

## Chapter 3: Voices from the Future

4. Press release, the Time Traveler Convention held at the Massachusetts Institute of Technology, May 7, 2005, http://web.mit.edu/adorai/timetraveler.

5. Press release, the Time Traveler Convention.

6. John Titor, "Civil War," John Titor Times, www.johntitor.com/pages/civilwar.html.

7. Quoted in Niburu, "Billy Meiers Earthquake Prediction Echoed by Scientists," Niburu, September 25, 2008, www.niburu.nl/index.php?articleID=19192.

8. Michael Taylor, "Billy Meier Exposed!" www.geocities.com/area51/corridor/8148/scam.html.

9. Taylor, "Billy Meier Exposed!"

## Chapter 4: Building a Time Machine

10. Quoted in PBS, "Time Travel," television episode of the series *NOVA*, airdate October 12, 1999, PBS, www.pbs.org/wgbh/nova/transcripts/2612time.html.

11. Paul Davies, "How to Build a Time Machine," Ana Sayfa, www.zamandayolculuk.com/cetinbal/buildtimetravel.htm, 2005.

# Glossary

**continuum:** A link between two things, such as time and space, that blend into each other so gradually it is impossible to find distance between them.

**dilation:** The process of something being widened or stretched.

**dimension:** The measurement of something such as height, length, width, or time.

**extraterrestrials (ETs):** Beings from another planet.

**nanosecond:** One billionth of one second.

**paradox:** A statement or situation that seems to contradict itself but is, in fact, actually true.

**physicists:** Scientists who specialize in physics, the science of time, space, matter, energy, and motion.

**science fiction:** Made-up stories that describe imaginary events and characters and that are loosely based on scientific concepts.

**skeptics:** People who question commonly held beliefs, especially about supernatural events.

**supernatural:** A being, like a ghost, or an event, like a time slip, that cannot be described by science or laws of nature.

# For Further Exploration

## Books

Mary Gribbin and John Gribbin, *Time & Space*. London: Dorling Kindersley, 2000. An Eyewitness Science book that explores the speed of light, time machines, the fourth dimension, and other related information.

John Hamilton, *Time Travel*. Edina, MN: ABDO, 2007. This book discusses time travel and the plots of classic books, movies, and TV shows.

Madeline L'Engle, *A Wrinkle in Time*. New York: Square Fish, 2007. Winner of the 1963 Newbery Medal, this is a classic time travel story about three children who get transported through the galaxy by means of the folding of the fabric of space and time.

Milton Meltzer, *Albert Einstein: A Biography*. New York: Holiday House, 2008. This biography explores the life and work of physicist Albert Einstein, awarded the Nobel Prize in Physics in 1921.

Jenny Randles, *Breaking the Time Barrier*. New York: Paraview Pocket Books, 2005. A book that details the history of people trying to build time machines, from the era of H.G. Wells to the 21st century.

## DVD

"NOVA: Einstein's Big Idea," DVD, directed by Gary Johnstone, PBS, 2005.

## Web Site

**NOVA—Time Travel** (www.pbs.org/wgbh/nova/time/). Companion site to NOVA's episode on Time Travel. Includes scientific perspectives on the possibility of time travel and the problems inherent in it.

# Index

# Picture Credits

# About the Author

Stuart A. Kallen has written over 250 books for children and young adults with topics ranging from astronomy to zoology. When not working on his next book, he can be found singing and playing guitar, or riding his bike along the beach in San Diego, California.